NELSON'S

WEST INDIAN READERS

Introductory Book

Compiled by J. O. Cutteridge

D0874847

OXFORD
UNIVERSITY PRESS

FOREWORD FOR TEACHERS

THIS book has been prepared to bridge the gap between the Infant Primers and Book I, and the subject matter now assumes an important aspect if the child is to read with intelligence and understanding. Every opportunity has therefore been taken to introduce local words and things with which the child is familiar.

The plan adopted is to present the word with a picture, the word being seen and learned as a whole, spelling being largely a visual exercise. The words are then used in simple sentences. The teacher should afterwards break up a few typical words into their parts on the blackboard to teach the sounds of the letters and their combinations, and they can then be combined again to form other similar words. Suggestions for this treatment are given as WORD STUDY, and teachers can add to the examples given.

"The primer must be graduated partly by considerations of phonetic difficulty; but this principle need not be carried to such an extent as to render the sentences meaningless or ridiculous. Nor need teachers be afraid of using an easy story-book because it contains occasional words presenting difficulty to the children. . . . Even if a word is not remembered from one occasion, it will recur probably a score of times during the next few years." (English Board of Education's "Suggestions.")

Emphasis should be laid on the *sounds* of letters. Examples for such phonic drill are given in red type. Analysis of words of two or more syllables into their parts presents difficulties to children at first. Systematic practice is given in this throughout the book.

J. O. CUTTERIDGE

LESSON 1

WORD-BUILDING EXERCISES

(For practice in phonic drill)

Note to Teacher.—The *sounds* of the letters printed in red should be revised, and then combined with the stems given to form words.

ack	ar	ark	ay	ade
back	car	bark	bay	made
pack	far	dark	day	wade
sack	star	hark	hay	shade
black		mark	may	
quack	art		nay	air
	cart	ame	say	fair
ash	dart	name	way	hair
dash	start	game	stay	chair
rash		same	play	
hash	ard		pray	ake
smash	hard			bake
	lard	alk	ail	make
	yard	talk	nail	take
ast		walk	pail	
fast	arn	chalk	sail	ale
last	barn			sale
mast	darn		ate	tale
		aw	late	whale
and	arm	saw	gate	
hand	farm	paw	slate	alf
sand	harm	claw	mate	calf
stand	charm	draw	hate	half
		papaw		

3

knife	fork	spoon
plate	bottle	glass
cup saucer	bowl	jug
food-carrier	coal-pot	sauce-pan

LESSON 2

THINGS WE USE

I cut my meat with a knife and hold it
with a fork.

We can stir our tea with a spoon.

Put your rice on a plate.

What is in that bottle?

I think there is milk in it.

Pour the milk into a glass.

There is a cup and a saucer.

Dip some water in the bowl for me.

The jug is empty.

I take my father's food in the food-
carrier.

The food has been cooked on the coal-
pot in a sauce-pan.

WORD STUDY

knife	fork	ice	spoon
knee	cork	rice	moon
know	pork	nice	coon
knew	emp-ty	mice	soon
car-ry	car-ri-er	sauce	sauc-er

table	chair	candle
lamp	flat-iron	chest
broom	bench	key
needle thread	thimble	scissors

6

LESSON 3
THINGS IN THE HOUSE

There is a chair by the table.
When it is dark we light a lamp or a
     candle.
My mother can press my dress with a
     flat-iron.
She folds it and puts it in the chest.
Where is the broom for me to sweep the
     house?
O, there it is under the bench.
Have you the key to unlock the box?
Mary wants a needle and thread as well
     as her thimble and scissors.
She is going to sew.

WORD STUDY

a-ble	oth-er	sweep	scis-sors
ta-ble	moth-er	swim	scythe
ca-ble	broth-er	swell	scent
una-ble	smoth-er	sweet	ir-on, key
thim-ble	nim-ble	can-dle	han-dle

hammer	saw	axe
hoe	rake	cutlass
barrow	cart	yoke
pannier	bridle	saddle

8

LESSON 4

IN THE GARDEN

Bring me the hammer and some nails.
I want to mend the gate.
I must split the wood with my axe as
I have no saw to cut it with.
Tom has cleaned the garden beds with
his hoe and rake.
Have you a cutlass to brush the path?
Here is a barrow to put the rubbish in.
The two oxen that pull the cart are fixed
to a yoke.
Let us ride down to the estate on the
ass. It has a bridle and saddle.
Look in the pannier. There are some
beans in it.

WORD STUDY

yoke	bri-dle	ar-row	pan-ni-er
poke	sad-dle	bar-row	rub-bish
spoke	la-dle	mar-row	es-tate
stroke	mid-dle	nar-row	cut-lass

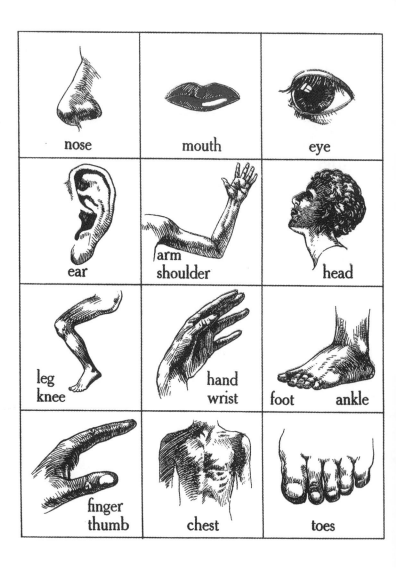

nose	mouth	eye
ear	arm shoulder	head
leg knee	hand wrist	foot ankle
finger thumb	chest	toes

LESSON 5
THE BODY

The parts of the body are the head, the trunk, and the limbs.

I smell with my nose, I see with my eyes, I hear with my ears, and I speak with my mouth. These are all parts of my head.

The arms and legs are called limbs. The shoulder is where the arm joins the trunk, and the ankle is where the foot joins the leg.

I can bend my leg at the knee, and my arm at the elbow and wrist.

There are four fingers and one thumb on each hand. Each foot has five toes.

The front of the trunk is called the chest.

WORD STUDY

limb	wrist	shoul-der	speak
climb	write	boul-der	beak
dumb	wrong	moul-der	teak
thumb	wreck	el-bow	leak
(*silent* "b")	(*silent* "w")	be-tween	fing-er

LESSON 6
MAKING WORDS

1. Write these words on your slate or book, and put an "e" at the end of each word:—

can	hop
cap	not
hat	car

Do you know the words you have made?

2. Write these words on your slate or book, leaving off the "e" at the end of each word:—

rate	cube
mate	hide
tube	pine

Make sentences with the new words you have made.

Write two sentences on your slate or book.

Write three more words which end in "e."

LESSON 7
WORD REVISION

Read these words. If you do not know some of them, turn back to the page on which they were found. Learn them again.

glass	pannier	swell
bench	ankle	candle
saddle	climb	going
mouth	wrong	narrow
whale	sentence	spoke
bottle	stand	ear
scissors	charm	wreck
cutlass	knife	shoulder
thumb	jug	leak
sail	carry	last
smash	thimble	wade
saucer	scythe	papaw
knee	unable	fork
chair	flat-iron	spoon
rake	barrow	coal-pot
toes	stroke	table
half	estate	needle
quack	write	brother
slate	speak	cable
bowl	tube	bridle
empty	finger	rubbish
thread	knee	eye
chest	mice	limb
sweep	broom	key

LESSON 8

COLOURS

Leaves and grass are green. Lemons are yellow. Mangoes are green, yellow, and red.

A banana is yellow, and so is the inside of a pineapple.

Salt is white, and paper is white; eggs are white outside and yellow inside.

The Johnny crow is black, and ink is black.

Coconuts are brown, and the earth is brown.

The sky is blue; the clouds in the sky are white and grey.

Some flowers are crimson, and others are pink.

The king has purple robes.

WORD STUDY

pur-ple	yel-low	flow-er	John-ny
cou-ple	mel-low	tow-er	pa-per
crum-ple	hol-low	bow-er	crim-son
dim-ple	fol-low	show-er	ba-na-na

The Rainbow

The rainbow has seven colours: red, orange, yellow, green, blue, very dark blue, and purple.

The cover of this book is red. Lemons are yellow and the sea is blue. Sometimes the sea is very dark blue, almost purple.

Can you name some things that are green in colour? What fruit is orange in colour?

We see colours with our eyes. Some colours are bright; others are dark. Some are tinted with white which makes them paler; others are shaded with black which makes them darker.

WORD STUDY

rain-bow	bright	shade	fruit
rain-coat	light	fade	suit
rain-cloud	night	tint	
rain-drop	sight	hint	

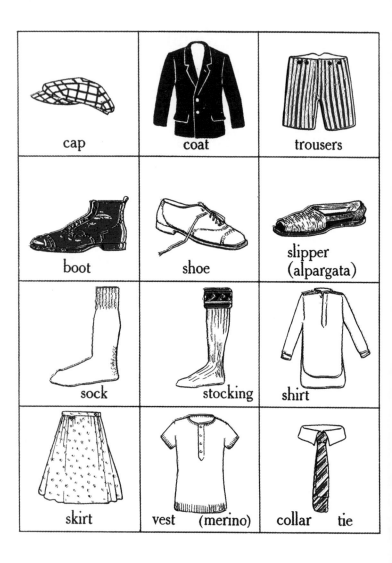

cap	coat	trousers
boot	shoe	slipper (alpargata)
sock	stocking	shirt
skirt	vest (merino)	collar tie

LESSON 9
THINGS WE WEAR

When we walk in the sun we cover our
heads.

A boy wears a cap or a hat, but a girl
has a hat.

Harry went to the store and fitted on
some boots and shoes.

He often wears slippers or alpargatas
on his feet.

Tom has stripes on his coat and trousers,
and Mary has spots on her skirt.

Tom's other clothes are a vest or merino,
a shirt, and socks or stockings.

He also wears a white collar and a red
tie.

WORD STUDY

dirt	wear	fit-ted	slip-pers
skirt	bear	bat-ted	al-par-ga-ta
shirt	pear	rot-ted	trou-sers
thirty	tear	pet-ted	col-lar

house	roof	floor
ajoupa	door	window
jalousie	wall	ceiling
steps	boards	fence

18

LESSON 10
THE HOUSE

Let us go into a house. Perhaps it is an ajoupa.

The roof is made of leaves, and the walls are made of mud.

Walk up the steps and open the door. One of the boards of the floor is broken.

There is a mat on the floor. We can sit on it.

It is very hot inside. Open the window or the jalousie to let in the fresh air.

Our school has a ceiling, but this house has none.

There is a strong fence round the garden.

WORD STUDY

aj-ou-pa	oar	door	fence
jal-ou-sie	roar	poor	pence
win-dow	boards	floor	hence
ceil-ing	coarse	bro-ken	whence

LESSON 11

SENTENCES TO FINISH

Can you put in the word needed to finish
each of these sentences?

I cut my meat with a ＿＿.
I stir my milk with a ＿＿.
I brush my hair with a ＿＿.
I wash my hands with a ＿＿.
I walk with my ＿＿.
I see with my ＿＿.
I hear with my ＿＿.

Mother sews with a ＿＿.
She sweeps with a ＿＿.
She irons with a ＿＿.

Father digs the garden with a ＿＿.
He brushes the path with a ＿＿.
He hammers a nail with a ＿＿.
He lights the fire with a ＿＿.

LESSON 12

WORD-BUILDING EXERCISES

(For practice in phonic drill as in Lesson 1)

eg	ee	ear	ing	ice
beg	see	dear	sing	nice
leg	three	fear	ring	mice
peg		hear	wing	spice
	eed	near	bring	slice
end	heed		string	ide
bend	need	eat	spring	side
lend	seed	beat		tide
send	weed	heat	ick	wide
mend		meat	pick	hide
	eep	seat	sick	slide
ent	deep		tick	ike
rent	keep	each	thick	like
sent	sleep	beach		strike
tent		teach	ilk	
went	een	reach	milk	ine
	seen	bleach	silk	fine
est	green			mine
best		in	ink	shine
rest	eel	pin	sink	
west	feel	sin	think	ire
nest	steel	thin	drink	fire
test	reel	tin	pink	tire

21

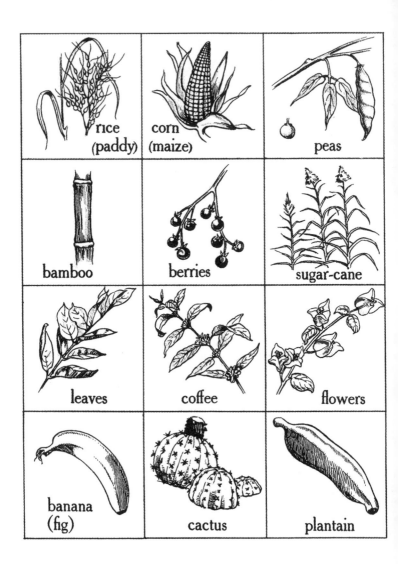

rice (paddy)	corn (maize)	peas
bamboo	berries	sugar-cane
leaves	coffee	flowers
banana (fig)	cactus	plantain

PLANTS

Plants grow in the ground. The sun and
the rain make them grow.

Rice or paddy likes much water on the
flat land.

We can plant our corn or maize on
hillsides.

Pigeon peas are good to eat with rice.

The bamboo is a very tall plant. It grows
quickly; so does the sugar-cane.

Most plants have leaves, and some have
flowers and berries, such as the
coffee plant.

Give me a banana or fig. I will take the
plantain home to cook it.

We do not eat the cactus. It has prickles.

WORD STUDY

ber-ry	ber-ries	pric-kle	su-gar
pen-ny	pen-nies	tic-kle	cac-tus
stor-y	stor-ies	buc-kle	cof-fee
fair-y	fair-ies	cac-kle	plan-tain

LESSON I4
WORD REVISION

Read these words as you did in Lesson 7:—

coat	shoe	hollow
sock	thirty	Johnny
house	slipper	couple
wall	wear	alpargata
teach	fitted	merino
think	boards	skirt
rest	ajoupa	trousers
bring	fence	pear
rice	broken	petted
peas	brushes	jalousie
blue	father	window
pink	steel	ceiling
stocking	heat	coarse
collar	three	school
floor	fire	hammer
steps	bamboo	bleach
green	corn	drink
silk	plantain	thin
shine	paddy	string
leaves	prickle	cactus
coffee	fairy	sugar-cane
orange	berries	maize
white	purple	stories
earth	grey	black

LESSON 15

THE MOUSE

A city mouse lives in a house;
  A garden mouse lives in a bower.
He's friendly with the frogs and toads,
  And sees the pretty plants in flower.

A city mouse eats bread and cheese;
  A garden mouse eats what he can.
We will not grudge him seeds and stalks,
  Poor little, timid, furry man.

CHRISTINA G. ROSSETTI

Where does a city mouse live?
Name two friends of the country mouse.
What does the city mouse eat?
Name two things the garden mouse eats.
Have you ever seen
  a mouse?
What colour was it?
Where was its home?
Which is larger—a
  rat or a mouse?

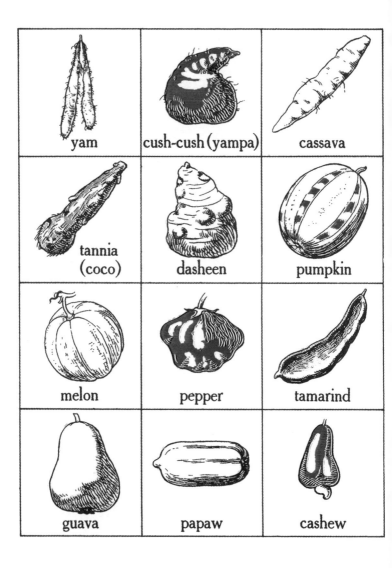

yam	cush-cush (yampa)	cassava
tannia (coco)	dasheen	pumpkin
melon	pepper	tamarind
guava	papaw	cashew

THINGS WE EAT

What do you like for your dinner?—
baked yam, boiled cush-cush, or
tannia cakes?

In your garden you may grow other
things to eat, such as cassava and
dasheen.

Your mother can make good soup from
a pumpkin. She makes it hot with a
red pepper.

Most fruits grow on trees. The papaw is
sweet and juicy, but the tamarind
has a sharp taste.

The cashew has its seed outside. We eat
cashew nuts after they are roasted.

Guava jelly is very sweet. It makes me
thirsty, and then I like to suck a
watermelon.

WORD STUDY

oil	roast	cash-ew	pump-kin
boil	toast	mel-on	gua-va
soil	coast	cas-sa-va	dash-een
toil	boast	fruit	tam-ar-ind

crab	lobster	spider
scorpion	centipede	lizard
snake	frog	toad
beetle	moth	butterfly

LESSON 17
LIVING THINGS WE KNOW

Things which are alive and can move
about are called animals.
Birds and bats fly in the air. Fishes,
frogs, and toads swim in water.
Land crabs live in holes in the ground.
Lobsters and sea crabs live in the sea.
The butterfly, the moth, and the beetle
have wings. They are insects.
The scorpion carries its tail over its
back.
It can sting; so can the centipede.
Snakes crawl along the ground. Some of
them give poison when they bite.
The spider spins its web to catch flies.
Lizards can run fast. They live on the
ground or in trees.

WORD STUDY

catch	car-ry	spi-der	cent-i-pede
match	car-ries	bee-tle	scor-pi-on
hatch	hur-ry	poi-son	liz-ard
scratch	hur-ries	an-i-mal	but-ter-fly

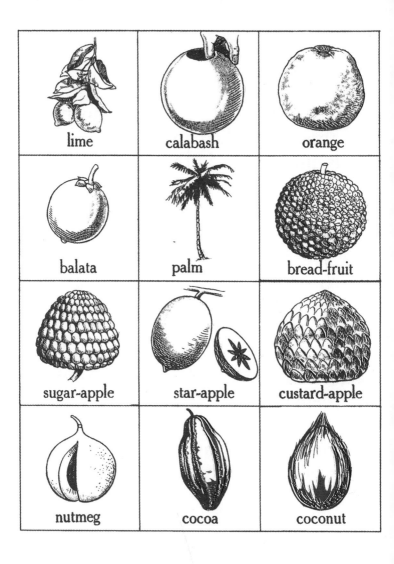

lime	calabash	orange
balata	palm	bread-fruit
sugar-apple	star-apple	custard-apple
nutmeg	cocoa	coconut

TREES

The roots of a tree are in the ground. We can see the trunk, branches, and leaves.

The coconut palm has a long straight stem. The cocoa, balata, and breadfruit trees have many branches.

Nutmeg is a spice. It grows on a tree. The mace is outside the shell.

Some fruits that we like to eat are sugar-apple, custard-apple, and star-apple. They have seeds inside them.

The juice of the orange is sweet, but that of the lime is sour or acid.

A calabash grows on a tree. We can make it into a basin to dip water.

WORD STUDY

range	mace	straight	ca-la-bash
or-ange	face	bought	ba-la-ta
change	race	fought	co-coa
strange	pace	caught	co-co-nut

LESSON 19
THE COCONUT

The coconut tree grows by the sea. It is tall, and has green leaves at the top.

The coconut is large and round. Its shell is hard and brown.

The meat is white. We may eat it. Here is a nut. We can see the meat inside the broken piece.

The water from the green nut is good to drink.

The nut has a husk made of fibre.

Here is a young tree.

It has not started to bear yet.

The nuts come after five years.

LESSON 20

WORD-BUILDING EXERCISES

(For practice in phonic drill as in Lesson, I)

ite	ob	ow	oot	ow
kite	cob	row	foot	cow
mite	rob	bow	boot	how
white	sob	sow	shoot	now
quite	knob	slow		sow
		grow	ood	
ight	ong	know	good	own
night	long	show	wood	down
fight	song		stood	town
light	wrong	old		crown
right		cold	ook	drown
sight	ond	gold	book	
bright	fond	sold	cook	our
	pond	told	look	hour
ind		hold	took	flour
bind	orn	ole	ool	
find	corn	hole	cool	ound
kind	born	pole	pool	found
mind	thorn	stole	tool	round
		cre-ole	school	sound
ore	oat			ground
more	boat	y	oon	
sore	goat	my	soon	ouse
store	coat	fly	moon	house
shore	float	sky	spoon	mouse

33

cow

zebu bull

goat

horse

donkey

mule

monkey

mongoose

rabbit

squirrel

turtle

agouti
(Indian rabbit)

LESSON 21
ANIMALS.—I

Some animals are useful to us. We can ride on the donkey or ass; the mule and the horse can pull heavy loads.

We get milk from the cow and the goat. The zebu bull can draw a cart.

Many other animals are wild. They live in the trees and bush. We catch some of them to eat.

The agouti and the lappe have good meat.

The monkey and the squirrel can climb trees, and the mongoose climbs a little. It eats young chickens.

The rabbit is a pet. It has soft fur.

The turtle is an animal which lives in the sea.

WORD STUDY

bar-rel	mule	wild	use-ful
squir-rel	rule	mild	care-ful
quar-rel	mon-goose	child	waste-ful
sor-rel	a-gou-ti	tur-tle	hope-ful

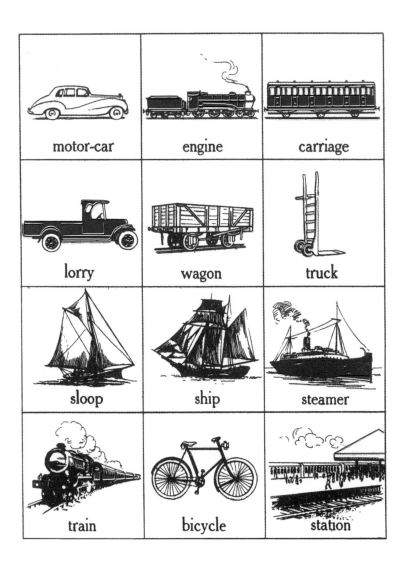

motor-car	engine	carriage
lorry	wagon	truck
sloop	ship	steamer
train	bicycle	station

LESSON 22
HOW WE TRAVEL

When we travel from one place to another we may walk or we may ride.

The motor-car can travel quickly. It has an engine in it.

A train has an engine at the front. It also has carriages for people and wagons for goods. It stops at the station.

Men take boxes to the store in a lorry or a truck.

Ships sail on the sea. A steamer has engines, but a sloop has sails. They bring things from other countries.

How many wheels has a bicycle? When you ride one you push the pedals.

WORD STUDY

ped-al	hoop	na-tion	mo-tor
med-al	coop	sta-tion	car-ri-age
lor-ry	loop	dicta-tion	en-gine
sor-ry	sloop	wa-gon	bi-cy-cle

LESSON 23

MORE SENTENCES TO FINISH

Can you finish these sentences?

The moon comes out at ——.
The sun rises in the ——.
The sun sets in the ——.
The flowers open in the ——.
The leaves of the coconut tree grow
    at the ——.

————————

Can you put in the missing word?

—— are good to eat.
Children love to play in the ——.
Mother rocks the —— to sleep.
The mongoose can ——.
We eat our —— in the morning.
I write in my ——.
Plantain is —— good to eat.
My book fell on the ——.

LESSON 24

SUGAR-CANE

The boys have a piece of sugar-cane.
They like to suck it. It has a sweet taste.

Sugar-cane grows in the sun. It is tall, and the stem is thick and heavy.

The juice of the cane is sweet and sticky. Sugar is made from it.

When it is crop-time we cut the cane, and send it to the mill to be ground. The oxen, mules, and donkeys pull the carts to the mills.

Here is a sugar factory where they grind cane.

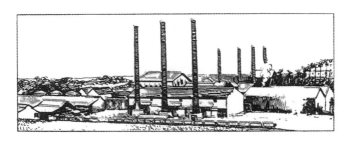

The box is square. The basket is round.

My square box is bigger than your round basket.

How many limes could you put in your box?

It will hold twelve or a dozen.

I can see your round basket on the square table.

What have you in your basket?

O, you have a mango and two bananas.

The mango is for a girl, and the bananas are for the boys.

———————

Here are the names of some more things which are round or square. Can you add to these lists?

Round—sun, moon, ball, a cent, orange, mango, bread-fruit.

Square—book, window, door, box, table, black-board.

WORD STUDY

square	twelve
squat	bas-ket
squir-rel	doz-en
black-board	big-ger

fowl (chicken)	duck	turkey
goose	pigeon	dove
parrot	hawk	macaw
owl	yellow-tail	boat-tail

42

BIRDS

Birds lay eggs. We eat the eggs of the hen, duck, goose, and turkey.

Some birds make their nests in trees. They build them of grass and twigs.

You can climb the trees and see the nests; but do not take the eggs.

The yellow-tail hangs its nest from the branch of a tree.

The macaw is a pretty bird, and so is the parrot. The boat-tail is black.

The owl flies at night. The hawk sometimes kills chickens.

Which bird flies very fast? The pigeon.

Which bird keeps near the ground? The dove.

WORD STUDY

key	goose	hen	pige-on
tur-key	geese	cock	ma-caw
don-key	owl	duck	par-rot
mon-key	fowl	drake	some-times

running	swimming	eating
sitting	standing	walking
writing	drawing	reading
drinking	sleeping	climbing

LESSON 27
THINGS WE DO

The man is climbing the coconut tree to pick the nuts.

We shall soon be drinking the water from the green nuts, and eating the meat from the ripe ones.

The fish is swimming in the sea.

I can see the horse running in the street.

The first boy is sitting on the bench. The second one is standing, and the third one is walking to school.

When he gets there he will be writing on his slate or reading from his book. He may be drawing on the wall.

Tonight he will be sleeping in his bed.

WORD STUDY

bark-ing	jump-ing	take	tak-ing	swim-ming
look-ing	weep-ing	bake	bak-ing	sit-ting
sing-ing	sell-ing	joke	jok-ing	run-ning
fly-ing	touch-ing	drive	driv-ing	bat-ting

(Note the omission of the "e" and the doubling of the consonant.)

LESSON 28

THE MISSING WORD

One of these words is needed in each of the sentences below—*clock, tree, motor-car, wind, and bamboo.*

Put each word in its right place.

1. A ____ has an engine, which makes it go. It runs on wheels, and can go very fast. It cannot climb trees or fences.

2. A ____ has a face and two hands. One hand is longer than the other.

3. The ____ is a tall grass. We make flower-pots from its hollow stem.

4. We can hear the ____ whistling through the trees.

5. A ____ has roots, leaves, and branches.

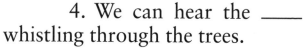

WHAT AM I?

I grow on a tall plant. My colour is green, and sometimes reddish.

At one end I am pointed, and at the other is the little stalk by which I am joined on to the plant.

Inside me there are many small seeds. You like to eat me when I am cooked. I am rather slimy then.

People boil me with crabs to make callaloo soup.

They mix me with corn-meal to make coo-coo.

Here is my picture.

I am an _____.

WORD STUDY

talk	red-dish	though
walk	sli-my	al-though
chalk	cal-la-loo	corn-meal
stalk	peo-ple	coo-coo

LESSON 30

THE MISSING WORD

Can you find the missing word?

1. Four little boys
    Were having some fun;
    ____ went away,
    And that left one.

2. Ten little boys
    Standing up straight;
    ____ sat down,
    Then there were eight.

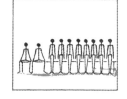

3. Eleven red mangoes
    High in a tree;
    Jim knocked down
    ____ of them,
    Then there were three.

4. Four yellow ducklings
    Walking in line;
    ____ more came walking,
    Then there were nine.

LESSON 31
PLANTAINS

Some plantain trees grow by the school. The long, wide leaves will shade you from the sun. You may also cover your head with them when it rains.

Plantains grow in a bunch.

We cut the tree down when the plantains are ripe. A new tree grows from a sucker.

We eat plantains. They can be boiled to eat with rice and salt fish, or we can fry them in a pan.

The plantain is a fruit. How many can you see below?

LESSON 32
WORD REVISION

Read these words:—

mouse	drake	cocoa
yam	reading	calabash
guava	drive	nutmeg
crab	joking	balata
toad	clock	coconut
moth	people	caught
lime	stalk	husk
palm	though	started
mace	salt-fish	mongoose
fibre	bunch	agouti
float	tannia	squirrel
bright	pepper	useful
store	cashew	wagon
know	cassava	engine
quite	roast	motor-car
goat	fruit	bicycle
mule	melon	sorry
sloop	spider	dictation
train	beetle	juice
crop-time	snake	factory
square	lizard	black-board
found	poison	twelve
hawk	animal	macaw
dove	scratch	pigeon

LESSON 33
MORE MISSING WORDS

The missing words on this page have the letters *ea* in each of them. Read the sentences, and put in the words which have been left out. Then write them on your slate or book.

1. Do not ____ animals with a stick.
2. Mother bought some ____ for dinner.
3. I did not ____ the lesson as I had no book.
4. There are some ____ in a motor-car.
5. I like to ____ a good story.
6. The sun rises in the ____.
7. Do not stand in the ____ of the run.
8. The school-master ____ me my lessons.
9. When I go home mother makes some ____ for me to drink.
10. There is a missing word in ____ of these sentences.

THE TIME OF DAY

Can you tell the time marked on these
  clocks?

Draw a clock face on your slate.

Put in the hands to, say, four o'clock.

Rub the hands off.

Make the clock say half-past six.

Rub the hands off again.

Make the clock say noon.

Note to Teacher.—Make a clock face from cardboard to illustrate
this lesson.

LESSON 35
WHAT AM I?

I am an animal. I live in the West Indies.

My tail is nearly as long as my body, but my legs are very short.

I eat birds, lizards, rats, and eggs. People put wire netting round their young chickens to keep me away.

I do not hunt at night, but only by day. I do not often climb trees.

My house is a little hole in the ground. I dig it myself.

You may often see me shoot across the road with my long tail straight out behind me.

Here is my picture. I am a ＿＿＿.

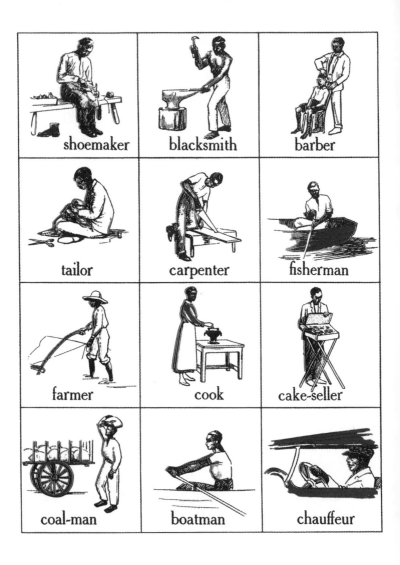

shoemaker	blacksmith	barber
tailor	carpenter	fisherman
farmer	cook	cake-seller
coal-man	boatman	chauffeur

WORK THAT PEOPLE DO

My father is a shoe-maker; when I grow older I want to be a blacksmith.

The tailor sews with his needle and thread. He makes clothes for us to wear.

The scissors of the barber are very sharp. He cuts my hair with them.

Who made the bench? The carpenter.

Many people help to get the food we eat. The farmer plants corn and rice.

The cook is cooking some red fish which the fisherman caught.

The coal-man makes coal in the woods to burn on the coal-pot.

Here comes the cake-seller. We can buy a nice cake for two cents, or a penny.

The chauffeur drives a motor-car.

WORD STUDY

aught	the	tail-or	shoe-mak-er
caught	bathe	sail-or	car-pen-ter
taught	lathe	cake-seller	fish-er-man
daught-er	clothes	black-smith	chauf-feur

LESSON 37
THE WIND

Who has seen the wind?
    Neither I nor you;

        But when the leaves hang
          trembling,
        The wind is passing
          through.

        Who has seen the wind?
          Neither you nor I;
        But when the trees bow
          down their heads,
        The wind is passing by.

CHRISTINA G. ROSETTI

Have you ever seen the
    wind?
Have you ever heard it
    crying or whistling?
How do you know when
    the wind is blowing?
Of what use is the wind?

56

LESSON 38
THE SEA AND FISH

Here we are on the blue sea. The boat sails with the wind. The waves ripple against its sides.
There are boys in the boat. They can see some fish in the sea.

The fisherman can catch fish with his line. He has hooks at the end of it.

The boys count the fish, and put them in a basket to take to the market.

The man has caught five. Here they are.

He wants seven more to make a dozen.

Can you draw a fish on your slate? Try to do so.

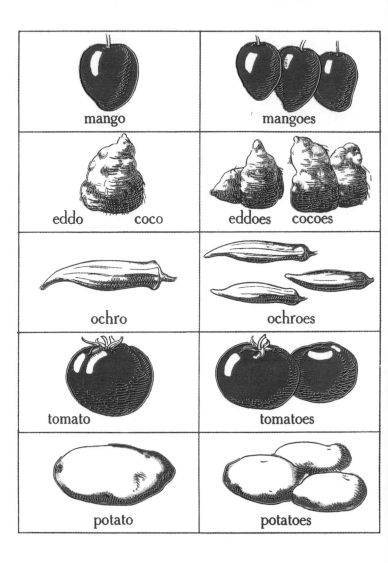

mango	mangoes
eddo coco	eddoes cocoes
ochro	ochroes
tomato	tomatoes
potato	potatoes

LESSON 39

ONE AND MORE THAN ONE

Look at the names under the pictures on page 58.

When the word means one thing it ends with the letter "o."

When it means more than one we add an "e" before putting on the "s."

Now let us read some of these words.

There are some mangoes in the basket. You can cut a mango with a knife.

The sweet potato grows in the ground, but tomatoes grow on a plant. They are red.

Ochroes have seeds inside them, but an eddo or coco is like a tannia.

All these things are good to eat.

There is another word which changes like those in this lesson.

It is a hard word, but one you know well. Learn to spell it.

Mos-qui-to.   Mos-qui-toes.

LESSON 40
SOMETHING TO DO

1. Spell slowly the word which you think is the hardest in this list: because, youngest, quick, pigeon, calabash.
2. Make three words out of these letters: t, e, s, a. You must use them all in each word. When you are ready stand.
3. Say the numbers backwards from ten to one.
4. Learn this so that you can say it without looking at your book. Stand when you are ready.

> "Twinkle, twinkle, little star,
> How I wonder what you are,
> Up above the world so high
> Like a diamond in the sky."

5. Name any other three rhymes you know.
6. Repeat one of these rhymes to the class.

LESSON 41

THE RAINBOW

Boats sail on the rivers,
   And ships sail on the seas;
But clouds that sail across the sky
   Are prettier far than these.

There are bridges on the
     rivers,
   As pretty as you please;
But the bow that bridges
     heaven
   And overtops the trees,
And builds a road from earth to sky,
   Is prettier far than these.

                  CHRISTINA G. ROSSETTI

Do you think you could learn to say this?
Ask your teacher to help you to learn it.
Do you think the twinkling star ever saw
    a prettier bridge than the rainbow?
Would you like it the best of all?

THE SUN, THE MOON, AND THE STARS

Is it morning? Yes, for the sun is shining.
The sun is bright and hot. Do not stand
     in the sun.
Always put a hat on your head when
     you go out in the sun.
The sun is round like a ball. See the
     large, round, golden sun in the sky.
It helps to make the plants grow.
The moon shines on the water. It is
     bright like silver.

The full moon is round. It rises late, but the new moon rises early.

See the new moon and the stars. The new moon is not round.

Is it morning? No, it is night. The stars are shining too.

I can see one moon, but I cannot count the stars.

WORD STUDY

gold-en	morn-ing	rise	sil-ver
whit-en	grow-ing	rises	al-ways
kit-ten	see-ing	raise	can-not
writ-ten	shin-ing	raises	wa-ter

A CIRCLE

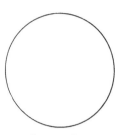

Do you know what this picture is?

Can you draw a circle on your slate?

Try to draw one.

A circle is harder to draw than a square.

Has a circle sides?

Did you ever draw a circle and try to make as many things as you could out of it?

Here are some of the things you might make by starting with a circle.

You might draw a hoop, the moon, a button, the sun, a cent, a face, a flower, an orange, or a cake of soap.

Write on your slate other things you could make out of a circle. Draw each one beside the name.

LESSON 44
RIGHT OR WRONG

Read each sentence to yourself as your teacher calls its number. If what it tells you is right, say "Right" when the teacher calls your name. If it is wrong, say "Wrong."

1. We make leather from the skins of ducks.
2. Our food is rice, salt-fish, and plantains.
3. Cows give us wool.
4. They give us milk too.
5. Hens lay eggs for us to eat.
6. Rice and yams grow on trees.
7. Fishes can run very fast.
8. We dig tannias out of the ground.
9. The cocoa tree has flowers.
10. They are large blue flowers.
11. The moon is square.
12. Mangoes are juicy.
13. We ride on animals or in carts.
14. Dogs build nests in trees.

LESSON 45
WORD REVISION

Read these words:—

bought	rainbow	count
lessons	bridges	basket
rises	teacher	potato
noon	shining	eddoes
marked	written	means
across	raise	changes
wire	always	rhyme
straight	circle	mosquito
tailor	wrong	centipede
barber	fishes	whiten
bathe	ochroes	cannot
taught	heard	early
neither	school-master	button
trembling	missing	leather
dozen	o'clock	flowers
ripple	netting	dasheen
market	picture	butterfly
mango	behind	lobster
tomatoes	carpenter	sugar-apple
changes	chauffeur	bread-fruit
twinkle	fisherman	turtle
because	daughter	sorrel
diamond	clothes	careful
quick	through	carriage

LESSON 46
WHAT AM I?

1.

I feed with worms my little ones,
    To make them big and fat;
Your babies cry for cakes and buns
    And funny food like that.

See, Jessie gives that baby boy
    A bowl of milk and bread;
I'm sorry that he can't enjoy
    A juicy worm instead.

                  I am a ____.

2.

There is one that has a head without an
    eye,
    And there's one that has an eye
    without a head;
You may find the answer if you try;
    And when all is said,
    Half the answer hangs upon a thread.

                CHRISTINA G. ROSSETTI

I am (1) a ____ and (2) a ____.

"SAVED" (H. Sperling)

LESSON 47
A PICTURE LESSON

Look at the picture on page 68. There are four animals in it. Three of them are dogs, and one is a cat.

They are near the steps of their master's house. We know the sun is shining, for we can see the shadows of the dogs on the ground.

This picture tells us a story. The two smaller dogs have been running after the cat. They had nearly caught it.

Near home it found a friend—its playmate, the large dog. The two enemies of the cat are afraid of him. They won't attack the cat now.

The picture is called "Saved." Why do you think it has this name?

WORD STUDY

won't	the master's house	en-e-my
don't	the dog's tail	en-e-mies
at-tack	the cat's fur	ba-by
sha-dow	the child's father	ba-bies

LESSON 48
PEPPERS

Peppers grow on a bush. They are red, brown, or green in colour; they are very hot to taste.

I can see some chilli peppers in this picture. Tiny flowers grow on the plant before it bears peppers.

We use peppers in cooking, and for making pepper-pot and hot sauce.

There are many kinds of peppers. Some are round and some are long. In the picture below I can see some bird-peppers and some cherry-peppers. Birds eat them.

LESSON 49

THE WEATHER

Harry and Jack liked the days when their teacher asked about the weather.

There were sentences about the weather on the black-board, and the children read each one to themselves. If it was true that day, they said "Right." If it was not true, they said "Wrong."

How would you like to try this game? Here are some of the sentences:—

1. The sun is shining.
2. There is no sunshine today.
3. The clouds are dark.
4. The clouds are white and pretty.
5. There is not a cloud in the sky.
6. The clouds cover the blue sky.
7. The stars are shining in the sky.
8. The moon is there too.
9. The wind is blowing strongly.
10. There is no wind.
11. The shadows of the trees are on the ground.

Uncle David gave Billy a picture book. It was filled with pictures of animals.

There were white bears on the ice in the cold land. There were lions looking so fierce that Betty turned the page quickly for fear they might roar.

But Betty liked best of all the page which had pictures of monkeys. Their funny little faces made her laugh.

The children would close the book, and ask each other questions to see how many animals they knew.

Here are some of the questions Billy asked Betty one night. How many of them can you answer?

1. What animal has a hump on its back?
2. Do you know an animal which can live under water?

3. What animal has wool
   on its back?
4. Which animal carries
   its trunk with it?
5. What animal has a nice shiny coat
   but no tail?

6. Do you know the
   animal which
   carries the beans
   to the cocoa-
   house?
7. What small animal
   has long ears
   which are pink
   inside?

8. Do you know an
   animal that likes
   chickens and eggs
   for its food?
9. There is a little animal which lives
   in trees. It carries its young ones
   on its back. What is it?
10. What animal has a spotted coat?
11. Which one can butt with its horns?

LESSON 51
THE DAYS OF THE WEEK

Is today Monday?
Is today Tuesday?
Is today Wednesday?
Is today Thursday?
Is today Friday?
Is today Saturday?
Is today Sunday?

What do you do on Saturday?
What do you do on Sunday?
What do you do on Monday, Tuesday,
    Wednesday, Thursday, and Friday?
Tell me the names of the days.
Do you notice that each one begins with
    a capital letter?

Will tomorrow be Monday?
Will tomorrow be Tuesday?
Will it be Saturday?
Will it be Sunday?
What day will tomorrow be?

What day of the week is this?
What day was yesterday?
What day comes after Wednesday?
What day comes after Thursday?
What day comes after Friday?

Do you know this verse about the days
of the week?—
"Monday's child is fair of face,
Tuesday's child is full of grace,
Wednesday's child is full of woe,
Thursday's child has far to go,
Friday's child is loving and giving,
Saturday's child works hard for its
living,
But the child that is born on Sunday
Is fair and wise and good and gay."

WORD STUDY

Sun-day	Tues-day	Fri-day
Mon-day	Wed-nes-day	Sat-ur-day
	Thurs-day	

SHOEING THE BAY MARE (*Landseer*)

LESSON 52
ANOTHER PICTURE LESSON

Look well at the picture, and it will help you to put in the words which are missed out in the lesson. One word is to go in each space.

The man is called a ____.

He has a ____ in his hand.

All the animals seem to be ____ at what the man is doing.

Perhaps there is a ____ in the cage.

The horse is standing very ____.

Donkeys and horses have shoes on their ____, but the ____ has not.

The tools are ____ the box.

The window of the smithy is ____, and the ____ is shining through.

The arm of the blacksmith looks very ____.

He is "____ the Bay Mare."

This is the ____ picture lesson in this book.

LESSON 53
TODAY, TOMORROW, AND YESTERDAY

Today	Tomorrow	Yesterday
I go to the village.	I shall go to the village.	I went to the village.
The boy learns his lessons.	The boy will learn his lessons	The boy learned his lessons.
Mary writes in her book.	Mary will write in her book.	Mary wrote in her book.
I drink my chocolate.	I shall drink my chocolate.	I drank my chocolate.
We are saying our tables.	We shall say our tables.	We said our tables.
The men are working on the estate.	The men will work on the estate.	The men worked on the estate.

This is the hottest day of the month. Crop-time begins today. You are sowing the seeds. The clock is ticking.	Tomorrow will be the hottest day of the month. Crop-time will begin soon. You will be sowing the seeds. The clock will be ticking.	Yesterday was the hottest day of the month. Crop-time began on Monday. You were sowing the seeds. The clock was ticking.

WORD STUDY

Today	Tomorrow	Yesterday
is walk-ing	will walk	walk-ed
is bark-ing	will bark	bark-ed
is call-ing	will call	call-ed
is look-ing	will look	look-ed
is laugh-ing	will laugh	laugh-ed
is say-ing	will say	said
is rid-ing	will ride	rode

IN THE TOWN

Betty and Tom live with their mother and father and sisters and brothers in a village in the country. Sometimes they go

to see their aunt and uncle and cousins in the town or city.

They like this very much, as they see many things there. In the streets there are many people walking and looking at the stores or shops, or going to the market.

The stores are full of pretty things. In the hardware store there are coal-pots, pans, brushes, pails, lamps, and food-carriers.

They can buy beautiful dresses and other clothes in the dry goods store, while at the grocery they can get all good things to eat and drink.

In the book-seller's shop there are books, pencils, pens, and ink-pots.

All kinds of medicine are sold at the drugstore.

People buy their meat and fish in the market, as well as fruits such as limes, mangoes, plantains, and oranges.

Betty and Tom like walking in the streets and looking at all these things.

In the big streets, too, there are tramcars. These run very fast, and they are full of people. Each has a bell, and it rings when the car is starting.

Children have to be careful when crossing the road, as there are so many

motorcars. People should always walk on the foot-path if there is one. SAFETY FIRST.

Betty likes to see the big ships in the harbour. Tom likes to see the trains with their big engines.

WORD STUDY

mo-ther	aunt	town	hard-ware
bro-ther	un-cle	ci-ty	gro-cer-y
fa-ther	cous-in	vill-age	med-i-cine
sis-ter	friend	coun-try	beau-ti-ful

THE UNION JACK

Red, white, and blue.

These are the colours of the British flag.

Red says, "Be brave."

White says, "Be pure."

Blue says, "Be true."

Let us think of this when we look at the
Union Jack.

It flies on many of the islands in the
West Indies.

We see it on Government House from
sun-rise to sun-set.

LESSON 56

MISSING LETTERS

In each of these words the red star shows where a letter is missing. What is it? Write the words, and put the missing letter in each one.

n*se	l*mes	un*le
l*g	b*x	w*ld
*ike	*ent	w*ter
f*el	a*s	*lso
h*ld	bul*	cra*
litt*e	vill*ge	inste*d
ju*cy	m*ngoose	w*ale
ans*er	*state	ch*ir
e*e	choc*late	p*paw
en*my	lau*hing	q*ack
bab*es	sa*d	sa*cer
pic*ure	br*ther	*nife
run*ing	tr*ins	j*g
an*mals	har*our	em*ty
pepp*rs	gro*ery	t*ree
t*ste	med*cine	s*oon
*lant	mango*s	thre*d
t*ny	t*ink	s*issors
cl*uds	plant*ins	i*on
bl*e	y*m	ke*
*rong	cous*n	pan*ier
dum*	fr*end	sad*le
*nee	a*nt	ham*er

w*ist	co*ntry	nar*ow
mon*ey	Wed*esday	rubb*sh
you*g	Sat*rday	ox*n
Tu*sday	be*utiful	sho*lder
sc*ool	colo*rs	to*s
noti*e	sal*te	*rite
sh*es	bre*d	spe*k
smith*	sor*y	car*y
ha*f	or*nge	c*stard
f*rk	mai*e	stra*ght
s*irt	mou*e	w*ite
trou*ers	tan*ia	*gouti
coll*r	cass*va	t*rtle
bat*ed	c*shew	*uarrel
aj*upa	mel*n	b*cycle
*eiling	tam*rind	mot*r
fen*e	ro*st	carr*age
bo*rds	gu*va	ste*mer
j*lousie	fru*t	slo*p
le*ves	pum*kin	ped*l
b*nana	dashe*n	wag*n
b*rries	m*th	fact*ry
c*ffee	li*ard	t*elve
pe*s	scorp*on	sq*are
fair*es	cent*pede	pi*eon
p*rple	po*son	t*rkey
gr*y	ca*ch	som*times
p*nk	hur*y	par*ot
e*rth	pa*m	clim*ing
c*uple	bal*ta	swim*ing
co*rse	calab*sh	whis*ling

POETRY TO READ AND LEARN

PUSS AND HIS DINNER

Pussy has finished his work long ago,
    And now he rests for the day;
While up and down his sweeping broom
    The little mice scamper and play.

They watch the cat as he sits asleep,
    They hear him snoring loud;
"He's asleep, dear children," says old Mother Mouse,
So the little ones come in a crowd.

"I'm afraid I see," says one big mouse,
    "That old cat's eye on me!"
"Nonsense!" says one of the little ones,
    "He's asleep. How could that be?"

Then pussy opens just one little eye.
    "Asleep?" he says, laughing. "Not me!"
He jumps and catches a fat little mouse.
    "It's time for my dinner," says he.

THE RAINDROPS' MESSAGE

The silver raindrops patter
    Upon the earth today;
Tap! Tap! Their knock is gentle,
    And this is what they say:

"Oh, little flowers, awaken,
    And open wide your door;
Come out, in pretty dresses,
    For spring is here once more."

LUCY DIAMOND

THE SPRING

A little mountain spring I found
    That fell into a pool;
I made my hands into a cup
And caught the sparkling water up—
    It tasted fresh and cool.

A solemn little frog I spied
    Upon the rocky brim:
He looked so boldy in my face
I'm certain that he thought the place
    Belonged by rights to him.

ROSE FYLEMAN
(*From* The Fairy Green, *by permission of the author,
and of Messrs Methuen and Co., Ltd*)

AT THE SEASIDE

When I was down beside the sea
A wooden spade they gave to me
    To dig the sandy shore.
My holes were empty, like a cup,
In every hole the sea came up
    Till it could come no more.

R. L. STEVENSON

FOREIGN LANDS

Up into the cherry tree
Who should climb but little me?
I held the trunk with both my hands
And looked abroad on foreign lands.

I saw the next door garden lie,
Adorned with flowers, before my eye,
And many pleasant places more
That I had never seen before.

I saw the dimpling river pass
And be the sky's blue looking-glass;
The dusty roads go up and down
With people tramping into town.

If I could find a higher tree
Farther and farther I should see,
To where the grown-up river slips
Into the sea among the ships,

To where the roads on either hand
Lead onward into fairy land,
Where all the children dine at five,
And all the playthings come alive.

R. L. STEVENSON

THE LAMB

Little Lamb, who made thee?
Dost thou know who made thee?
Gave thee life, and bade thee feed,
By the stream, and o'er the mead;
Gave thee clothing of delight,
Softest clothing, woolly, bright;
Gave thee such a tender voice,
Making all the vales rejoice?
Little Lamb, who made thee?
Dost thou know who made thee?

WILLIAM BLAKE

THE NEST

A little bird sat on a bough.
He sat and sang: "I'm happy now;
The cold, cold wind has gone to bed;
The sun is shining overhead,
And shining on a little nest,
And on a bird with browny breast."

"Where is your nest?"
    "Ah: no one knows,
But two little birds
    And a briar rose."

MARGARET ASHWORTH

THE BROOK

I like to watch the merry brook
    Go rippling on its way;
It sings me such a happy song
    All through the summer day;
It tells me tales of many things,
    As on the grass I lie,
About the hills from which it came,
    And where it goes—and why.
And if I had a tiny boat,
    A-sailing I would go,
And hasten with the brook to join
    The river deep and slow.

LUCY DIAMOND

THE MOON

The moon has a face like the clock in the hall;
She shines on thieves on the garden wall,
On streets and fields and harbour quays,
And birdies asleep in the forks of the trees.

The squalling cat and the squeaking mouse,
The howling dog by the door of the house,
The bat that lies in bed at noon,
All love to be out by the light of the moon.

But all of the things that belong to the day
Cuddle to sleep to be out of her way;
And flowers and children close their eyes
Till up in the morning the sun shall rise.

R. L. STEVENSON

JEMIMA

There was a little girl, and she wore a little curl
  Right down the middle of her forehead;
When she was good, she was very, very good,
  But when she was bad, she was horrid.

MY LITTLE DOG

I'll never hurt my little dog,
  But stroke and pat his head;
I like to see him wag his tail,
  I like to see him fed.

Poor little thing, how very good,
  And very useful too;
For do you know that he will mind
  What he is bid to do?

Then I will never hurt my dog,
  And never give him pain,
But treat him kindly every day,
  And he'll love me again.

THE JUMBLIES

They went to sea in a Sieve, they did,
  In a Sieve they went to sea:
In spite of all their friends could say,
On a winter's morn, on a stormy day,
  In a Sieve they went to sea!

And when the Sieve turned round and round,
And every one cried, "You'll all be drowned!"
They called aloud, "Our Sieve ain't big,
But we don't care a button! we don't care a fig!
     In a Sieve we'll go to sea!"
       Far and few, far and few,
Are the lands where the Jumblies live;
Their heads are green, and their hands are blue,
And they went to sea in a Sieve.

They sailed away in a Sieve, they did,
   In a Sieve they sailed so fast,
With only a beautiful pea-green veil
Tied with a riband by way of a sail,
   To a small tobacco-pipe mast;
And every one said, who saw them go,
"Oh, won't they be soon upset, you know!
For the sky is dark and the voyage is long,
And happen what may, it's extremely wrong
     In a Sieve to sail so fast!"
       Far and few, far and few,
Are the lands where the Jumblies live;
Their heads are green, and their hands are blue,
And they went to sea in a Sieve.

The water it soon came in, it did,
   The water it soon came in;
So to keep them dry, they wrapped their feet
In a pinky paper all folded neat,
   And they fastened it down with a pin.
And they passed the night in a crockery-jar,

And each of them said, "How wise we are!
Though the sky be dark, and the voyage be long,
Yet we never can think we were rash or wrong,
    While round in our Sieve we spin!"
        Far and few, far and few,
Are the lands where the Jumblies live;
Their heads are green, and their hands are blue,
And they went to sea in a Sieve.

And all night long they sailed away;
    And when the sun went down,
They whistled and warbled a moony song
To the echoing sound of a coppery gong,
    In the shade of the mountains brown.
"O Timballo! How happy we are,
When we live in a Sieve and a crockery-jar,
And all night long in the moonlight pale,
We sail away with a pea-green sail,
    In the shade of the mountains brown!"
        Far and few, far and few,
Are the lands where the Jumblies live;
Their heads are green, and their hands are blue,
And they went to sea in a Sieve.

EDWARD LEAR

THE CATS' TEA-PARTY

Five little pussy-cats, invited out to tea,
Cried: "Mother, let us go—Oh, do! for good we'll
    surely be.

We'll wear our bibs and hold our things as you have
 shown us how—
Spoons in right paws, cups in left—and make a pretty
 bow;
We'll always say, 'Yes, if you please,' and 'Only half of
 that.'"
"Then go, my darling children," said the happy Mother
 Cat.
The five little pussy-cats went out that night to tea,
Their heads were smooth and glossy, their tails were
 swinging free;
They held their things as they had learned, and tried to be
 polite,—
With snowy bibs beneath their chins they were a pretty
 sight

But alas, for manners beautiful, and coats as soft as silk
The moment that the little kits were asked to take some
 milk,
They dropped their spoons, forgot to bow, and oh, what
 do you think?
They put their noses in the cups and all began to drink!
Yes, every naughty little kit set up a miou for more,
Then knocked the tea-cups over, and scampered through
 the door.

F. E. WEATHERLEY

THEY SAY

They say we ought to love the rain
That beats upon the window-pane;
They say it makes the green grass grow,
And all the little rivers flow.
That's all very well, but what of me?
It doesn't make me grow, you see!

They say the rain will soon be o'er,
Then we can play upon the shore,
But hours and hours have passed away
Since it began to rain to-day.
If it were kind, I think it might
Rain only in the dark of night.

Suppose it didn't stop at all,
But day by day we saw it fall,
Until it covered up the ground
And there was water all around:
Why, then, we'd sail across the park,
Like Noah, in another Ark.

TENNYSON

OXFORD
UNIVERSITY PRESS

Great Clarendon Street, Oxford, OX2 6DP, United Kingdom

Oxford University Press is a department of the University of Oxford.
It furthers the University's objective of excellence in research, scholarship,
and education by publishing worldwide. Oxford is a registered trade mark of
Oxford University Press in the UK and in certain other countries

Text © J. O. Cutteridge 2013
Original illustrations © Oxford University Press 2014

The moral rights of the authors have been asserted

First published by Thomas Nelson and Sons in 1925
Second edition published by Nelson Thornes Ltd in 2013
This edition published by Oxford University Press in 2014

All rights reserved. No part of this publication may be reproduced,
stored in a retrieval system, or transmitted, in any form or by any
means, without the prior permission in writing of Oxford University
Press, or as expressly permitted by law, by licence or under terms
agreed with the appropriate reprographics rights organization.
Enquiries concerning reproduction outside the scope of the above
should be sent to the Rights Department, Oxford University Press, at
the address above.

You must not circulate this work in any other form and you must
impose this same condition on any acquirer

British Library Cataloguing in Publication Data
Data available

978-1-4085-2351-3

10 9 8 7 6 5 4

Printed in India

Acknowledgements

Page make-up: Compuscript Ltd

The author and the publisher would also like to thank the following for permission to
reproduce material:

Images
p76: Blacksmith, Landseer, Sir Edwin (1802-73) (after) / Private Collection / © Look and
Learn / The Bridgeman Art Library

Although we have made every effort to trace and contact all
copyright holders before publication this has not been possible in all
cases. If notified, the publisher will rectify any errors or omissions at
the earliest opportunity.

Links to third party websites are provided by Oxford in good faith
and for information only. Oxford disclaims any responsibility for
the materials contained in any third party website referenced in
this work.